Resource Guide for Towing Industry Support Professionals

Preparation Material for the Towing & Recovery Support
Certification Program® (TRSCP®)
Entry Level Exam

By Towing and Recovery Association of America, Inc.®
(TRAA)

Acknowledgments

The Towing & Recovery Support Certification Program® (TRSCP®) was developed from 2017-2018 with the support and grant funding of the U.S. Department of Transportation's Federal Highway Administration (FHWA). The TRSCP® is the first program of its kind within the incident management community.

The Towing and Recovery Association of America, Inc.® expresses its gratitude to the Women of the Towing & Recovery Association of America (WTRAA) for sharing their concept, FHWA for their continued support, and the dedicated professionals within the towing and recovery industry who served on the TRSCP® Advisory Committee. Without their time, energy, and expertise the TRSCP® would still just be an idea. Thank you on behalf of the entire industry and the professionals this program is intended to service.

TRSCP® Advisory Committee

John Borowski, Committee Member

Byron Harris, Committee Member

Kyle Herring, Committee Member

Cynthia Martineau, Committee Advisor

Elizabeth Martineau-Dupuis, Committee Chair

Lee Roberts, Committee Member

Gay Rochester, Committee Member

Geri Roskopf, Committee Member

Background

TRAA is publishing this guide as a resource for those working in the towing and recovery industry who are not themselves towing operators. Additionally, this guide may be used a study guide to prepare for the TRSCP® Entry Level certification exam.

As a professional certification program, the Towing & Recovery Support Certification Program® (TRSCP®) is intended to measure certain basic knowledge, skills, and competencies that have been deemed appropriate for those employed in support staff roles within the towing and recovery industry. These roles include dispatchers, office managers, administrative staff, etc. Participants must demonstrate that they meet these predetermined standards by successfully completing the corresponding assessment with a final score of 75% or higher. Certification evaluates knowledge but does not address or attempt to evaluate the participant's actual job performance.

The Towing & Recovery Support Certification Program® (TRSCP®) is owned by, the intellectual property of, and its materials under Copyright by the Towing and Recovery Association of America, Inc.® (TRAA). As such, none of its materials or likeness may be used without the written permission of TRAA. This guide is intended for educational purposes only.

Contents

1 Introduction

It is estimated that traffic incidents account for more than half of the traffic congestion in urban areas across the United States. The safe, quick, and effective clearance of traffic saves time, money, and the lives of motorists and responders. The major disciplines in Traffic Incident Management (TIM) are law enforcement, fire and rescue, emergency medical services, transportation, and towing and recovery professionals. Towing and recovery professionals are one of the only private sector partners on the TIM team. Visit the TIM website for more information: https://ops.fhwa.dot.gov/eto_tim_pse/about/tim.htm.

For towing and recovery professionals to effectively do their jobs, they rely on other industry professionals serving in supportive roles who are not themselves tow operators. While many don't work directly on the roadways, support personnel such as dispatchers, scene safety supervisors, compliance directors, and office managers are an integral part of the towing and recovery team. Agencies across the country recognize the need for trained and certified professionals to efficiently practice Incident Management (IM) and clear incidents in a timely manner.

The Towing & Recovery Support Certification Program® (TRSCP®) was developed as a national certification for individuals that provide support to incident management efforts but are not themselves tow truck operators. The role of support personnel is critical to effective incident management. Many of these individuals respond to incident sites or work behind the scenes to dispatch equipment and resources that are necessary to facilitate the clearance. They also handle communication, documentation, and track the incident for safety compliance thereby contributing to quick clearance needs.

While the TRSCP® was developed specifically for the towing and recovery industry, the program is open to all qualified candidates in other associated fields that meet the requirements. If you are an agency dispatcher in law enforcement, 911, TIM, Department of Transportation (DOT), etc. we hope this program will enhance your understanding of the equipment, resources, and logistics necessary for an efficient towing and recovery response and, thereby, increase interdisciplinary communication. If you are a non-agency party that may be present at an incident scene (such as Public Information Officers (PIO), media, fleet safety directors, and insurance adjusters), we hope this will expand your knowledge base of incident management and quick clearance.

Regardless of the specific role, we hope that reading the study guide and passing the corresponding certification exam will fill you with a sense of accomplishment and confidence in the important part you play in improving the efficiency of incident clearance, decreasing roadway congestion, and increasing safety for both responders and the motoring public.

2   Customer Service

One of the most important aspects of a support staff's role is customer service. Customer service is the act of taking care of a customer, client, or patron's needs by delivering professional, helpful, high quality assistance before, during, and after the customer's requirements are met. As a customer service agent, you are often the only communication point the customer has with the company. You are the voice and face of the company.

Excellent customer service can differentiate your company from its competitors and generate repeat business. On the other hand, poor customer service can lose customers, diminish public goodwill, and decrease employee morale. The importance of good customer service cannot be overstated; a company cannot survive without it.

2.1   Internal and External Customer Service

As support staff you will find customers don't only include people who enter your establishment or call for towing, recovery, or other vehicle services. Customers also include those who work every day to make the operations of a business successful – your fellow employees and team members. While external and internal customers may fulfill different roles, both are critical to the viability of the business and your role as a towing and recovery support staff.

An **external customer** is loosely defined as the "end user". They are not part of your organization and they typically pay your company for services. External customers are essential to the success of any business. At any time, an external customer can be law enforcement, business owners, motor clubs, private citizens, other tow companies, auto auctions, or insurance companies. One incident can have multiple customers. External customers typically have the choice of which company they patron. You want to establish a relationship built on trust and confidence which will generate positive reviews and make them a repeat customer.

An **internal customer** is any member of the organization who relies on assistance from another team member to fulfill their job duties. The best example of an internal customer would be the tow operator, they rely on you as the support staff to do their jobs effectively. They rely on you to relay appropriate information such as an incident's location, equipment required, etc. Note, while our incident management (IM) partners work in separate organizations, each partner depends on the other to accomplish the task of clearing the roadway and getting home safely. For this reason, our IM partners can become an internal customer in certain situations.

2.2   Best Practices

It is important for towing and recovery support staff to provide great customer service to both internal and external customers. Here are some best practices:

- **Pay Attention**: Internal and external customers expect and deserve your full attention and total concentration. Quickly set aside distractions or any tasks not related to servicing the customer. If in-person, make eye contact and acknowledge them right away with a warm greeting and a smile.

- **Communicate Clearly**: Choose your words carefully and make them positive and professional. Avoid slang, take care to enunciate, and don't talk too fast. Clear responses will help to prevent misunderstandings. Your words and the tone of your voice send a message about the quality of your service.

- **Ask Questions**: Ask questions to interpret, analyze, and anticipate the situation and how you may help.

- **Take Notes**: Write down important information and keep up-to-date notes. Notes, should include the date/time of communication, who you spoke with, and a brief description of the content. Having the information available will minimize customer confusion and frustration.

- **Know Your Resources**: Keep regular resources handy for easy access and know where to refer customers when needed.

- **Take Ownership**: Apologize for any mistakes and provide solutions, not excuses.

- **The Golden Rule**: Treat customers as you wish to be treated; with respect, courtesy, and consideration.

- **Attitude**: Customers appreciate a friendly and helpful approach and are put off by a negative one. You choose which attitude you bring to the interaction.

2.3   Conflict Resolution

Unfortunately, managing conflict is an element of customer service. Many customers you'll deal with are having a bad day and tensions are running high. If there is a disagreement, address the situation quickly, stay open-minded, and be courteous. All complaints should be taken seriously. Take detailed notes including the customer's name, contact information, and an account of the issue. Follow your company's established escalation policy and refer the customer to the next designated person such as your manager.

The most effective approach with complaints is to keep them from happening in the first place. Be proactive and inform customers about delays as soon as they arise. Some variables are out of your control, such as the weather, nonetheless customers will appreciate your honest and transparent feedback.

Whether it's a conflict with a tow operator (internal customer) or a private citizen (external customer) it can be difficult to stay calm during stressful situations. A few deep breaths can go a long way toward reducing tension on the spot. Understand that you have a stressful job and incorporate ways to minimize stress daily; make time for exercise, a hobby, or another healthy and relaxing activity that you enjoy.

3   Pre-Incident

3.1   Incident Types

Regardless of your specific role as a towing and recovery support staff, background knowledge of motor vehicle incidents is key. A motor vehicle incident can occur under any condition and for a variety of reasons. While each and every incident is unique, we can identify them by a few common variables. Knowing these general classifications is important for the quick identification of an incident's type and the special considerations that may be required when responding.

According to the National Highway Traffic Safety Administration's (NHTSA) 2015 Traffic Safety Facts, nearly all motor vehicle incidents fall into four categories[1]:

1. **Collision with Another Motor Vehicle:** The three most commonly reported occurrences within this category include rear-end collisions, angled impacts, and sideswipes.

   o A **rear-end collision** occurs when one vehicle collides into the back of the vehicle in front of it.

   o A **"T-bone" or "broadside" collision** has an angled impact. These occur when one vehicle strikes another at an angle, impacting the side of the vehicle.

   o A **sideswipe** incident occurs when the sides of two parallel cars touch and "swipe" each other.

   o A **head-on collision** is when two vehicles travelling in opposite directions collide, causing the front of one vehicle to impact the front of another.

---

[1] (National Highway Traffic Safety Administration, 2015)

Collisions involving multiple motor vehicles require special consideration when dispatching a recovery unit(s). Because of the nature of these collisions, vehicles involved in these types of incidents are often disabled in a variety of different ways. This means that one type of recovery vehicle, such as a medium duty flatbed truck or light duty wrecker, may be able to tow one vehicle involved but not another.

2. **Collisions with a Fixed Object**: These incidents occur when a motor vehicle impacts a stationary or fixed object such as a light post, curb, ditch, or guard rail.

3. **Collisions with a Non-Fixed Object**: These incidents occur when a motor vehicle impacts a stationary object that is not fixed in its position. According to the NHTSA, this occurs most often when a vehicle impacts a parked or disabled motor vehicle, animal, or pedestrian.

Collisions with both fixed and non-fixed objects more often than not cause damage to the front of the vehicle. Depending on the severity of the collision, it can also place the vehicle in an unusual position or angle. These are both important considerations when thinking through the recovery needs of an incident.

4. **Roll Overs**: These occur any time a vehicle leaves its wheels and is flipped or rolled onto its side or top. All three of the collision categories mentioned above may cause this type of incident. It is important to distinguish a roll over, however, because of the unique recovery techniques required. During a roll over, towing and recovery specialists are often asked to lift and flip the vehicle, returning it to its proper orientation to enable easier recovery and possibly rescue. Depending on the vehicle's size and weight, this may require highly specialized equipment and a longer recovery time.

Motor Vehicle Incident Types

Collision With a Motor Vehicle

Rear-end Collision

When one vehicle collides into the back of the vehicle in front of it.

Angled Impact (T-Bone or Broadside)

When one vehicle strikes another at an angle, impacting the side of the vehicle.

Sideswipe

When the sides of two parallel cars touch and "swipe" each other.

Head-on Collision

When two vehicles travelling in opposite directions collide, causing the front of one vehicle to impact the front of another.

Collision With an Object

Collision with a Fixed Object

When a motor vehicle impacts a stationary or fixed object such as a light post, curb, ditch, or guard rail.

Collision with a Non-Fixed Object

When a motor vehicle impacts a stationary object that is not fixed in its position like a parked or disabled motor vehicle, animal, or pedestrian.

Rollover

Any time a vehicle leaves its wheels and is flipped or rolled onto its side or top.

Towing and Recovery Support Certification Program™
Towing and Recovery Association of America, Inc.®

These incidents may involve a single vehicle, two vehicles, or occur multiple times within a single incident and involve several vehicles. This is referred to as a multi-car incident. It is also important to know that any vehicle, regardless of size or weight, may be involved in any one of the above-mentioned incidents.

In addition to incidents, towing and recovery companies may receive calls for other types of services including:

- **Winch Outs**- pulling a vehicle from a roadside area that is not easily accessible such as mud, sand, snow, and other inoperable substances.

- **Service Calls**- calls to assist the vehicle operator with issues such as lock-outs, flat tires, out of gas, jump starts, or other mechanical failures. Service calls may transition to a towing service based on the severity of the issue and/or location of the service call.

The Towing and Recovery Association of America, Inc.® (TRAA) recognizes three different general classifications of vehicles based on size and weight. They are light duty, medium duty, and heavy duty[2]:

1. **Light duty vehicles** may include passenger cars, light trucks, minivans, full-sized pickups, and sport utility vehicles.

2. The **medium duty** category includes a wide range of mid-sized vehicles such as delivery trucks, motorhomes, ambulances, flatbed trucks, box trucks, and small transit buses.

3. Finally, **heavy duty** vehicles include large delivery trucks, refuse or garbage trucks, cement mixers, and all tractor trailers.

---

[2] (Towing and Recovery Association of America, Inc., 2014)

For more information, please reference TRAA's Law Enforcement Vehicle Identification Guide©.

3.2   Special Considerations: Vehicle Types

Each vehicle manufactured is unique and some require special consideration; including hybrid cars, low-stance vehicles like sports cars, and any vehicle transporting a heavy or unique payload.

- **Hybrid Vehicles**: Since hybrid vehicles run, at least in part, on electricity, their batteries carry a very high voltage. An incident could potentially expose wires and put the tow operator at a unique risk of electric shock. Electric batteries are also in danger of setting fire. For these reasons, it is important for the tow operator to know the type of vehicle before approaching. High voltage lines are most often denoted by an orange or blue covering, but the vehicle specific operator's manual should always be consulted first.

- **Sports Cars and Modified Vehicles**: Sports cars and modified vehicles that sit particularly low to the ground may require special care when loading onto a tow truck as to not cause further damage to the vehicle.

- **Heavy Payloads:** Special care should also be taken when recovering a vehicle with unique or heavy payloads. Shifts in weight distribution can cause sudden and unexpected movements of a vehicle, putting the entire recovery crew at risk. Some payloads may be more fragile or hazardous than others and the driver/owner should always be consulted.

3.3   IM Partners: Defining Roles

Efficient and proper traffic incident management (TIM) requires a multidisciplinary approach designed to restore traffic capacity as safely and quickly as possible. It should be a coordinated process that involves a number of public and private sector partners. These partners include: law enforcement, fire and rescue, emergency medical services (EMS), transportation (DOT), public works, and towing and recovery. By understanding each partner's role during incident management, support staff can better assist their operators in the field.

Law enforcement agencies include State Police and Highway Patrols, County Police and County Sheriffs, Township and Municipal Police, and other agencies which have officers sworn to enforce laws. On the scene of a traffic incident the duties of these officials include: securing the incident scene, providing emergency medical aid until help arrives, safeguarding personal property, conducting incident investigations, supervising scene clearance, assisting disabled motorists, and directing traffic. Jurisdiction of law enforcement agencies varies widely across the country and within each state. Typically, state police and highway patrols have jurisdiction on state highways while county and municipal police have jurisdiction on roads outside the state highway system. Because jurisdiction varies greatly, it is important to always know how your local law enforcement jurisdiction is structured.

Fire and rescue services are provided by county and municipal fire departments, and by surrounding fire departments through mutual aid agreements. Typical roles and responsibilities at traffic incidents assumed by fire departments include: protecting the incident scene, suppressing fires, serving as incident commander for fire and rescue scenarios, providing emergency medical care, providing initial HAZMAT response and containment, rescuing crash victims from contaminated environments and wrecked vehicles, arranging transportation for the injured, assisting in incident clearance, and providing temporary traffic control until law enforcement or Department of Transportation (DOT) arrival.

In most jurisdictions, the fire department is the primary emergency response agency for hazardous material spills. In most large urban areas, full-time personnel staff fire and rescue departments. Whereas in many suburban and in most rural areas, fire and rescue services are primarily provided by volunteers.

The primary responsibilities of **EMS** are the triage, treatment, and transport of crash victims. In many areas, fire and rescue companies provide emergency medical services. In others, secondary agencies or private companies provide these services to local jurisdictions under contract. Typical roles and responsibilities assumed by EMS at traffic incidents include: providing advanced emergency medical care, determining the destination and transportation requirements for the injured, coordinating evacuation with fire, police, and ambulance or airlift, serving as incident commander for medical emergencies, determining approximate cause of injuries for the trauma center, and removing medical waste from the incident scene.

Transportation and public works agencies are essential for the safe and efficient managing of traffic in and around a traffic incident management area. Transportation and public works personnel possess specialized training, experience, and equipment for the advanced warnings, lane closures, and detour guidance needed to manage and direct traffic around or through an incident scene. These functions are essential for creating a safe working environment for other IM partners and mitigate many factors leading to secondary incidents. Transportation and public works technicians are also responsible for the operation and maintenance of traffic signals, signs, and roadway lighting involved in an incident.

3.4   Special Considerations: HAZMAT

A motor vehicle of any size or classification may be carrying hazardous materials. Towing and recovery service providers are responsible for the safe and efficient removal of wrecked or disabled vehicles, protecting and transporting victims' property and vehicles, and removing debris from the incident scene. They also provide other services such as temporary traffic control, rescue support, and HAZMAT containment and clean up as directed by contract, incident command, or specific contract requirements.

3.5 Situational Awareness

Situational awareness is the continual observation of a specific environment and how any change in that environment affects one's mission and safety. Situational awareness is essential for tow operators in the field who are dealing with changing and often dangerous circumstances. A high level of situational awareness is also critical for efficient, effective, and safe support staff function.

On any given day, a number of constantly changing variables could impact a towing and recovery operation. These could include weather, changes in traffic patterns, special events, roadway construction and lane closures, or even an area's geography. Each one of these variables has a unique impact on an incident response. By knowing how each one affects the response effort in advance, a support staff member can better assist the operators in the field.

To maintain a high level of situational awareness, towing and recovery support staff should first understand their baseline. That is, what is normal for a given time of day? By understanding how typical call volume and traffic ebbs and flows throughout the day, you can better determine how to adjust when a variable arises such as weather or a construction zone.

3.5.1 Geography

You should always know the geography of your towing jurisdiction so that you can quickly identify the closest and most appropriate response units based on the incident's location. When learning the physical geography of an area you should look for landmarks such as hills, bridges, fields, and ditches as well as man-made objects like shopping centers, intersections, bridges, overpasses, and unique buildings. These features serve as reference points for both office staff and the operators on the road.

Many of these features pose unique dangers to drivers and could be hot spots for incident activities. This is particularly evident at busy intersections or areas with high pedestrian traffic like office parks or transit stations. It is important to understand not just where these markers are, but how the geography affects the traffic flow and volume around them. For example, densely populated areas are more likely to experience an increase in traffic during peak rush hour times. This not only has the potential to slow response times based on the direction of the backup but may also increase your call volume.

Understanding your local roadway infrastructure is another important factor in establishing your situational awareness baseline. Many bridges and overpasses have height restrictions that could limit or divert responding units. By knowing the height restrictions of your fleet and the restrictions present in your jurisdiction, you can more effectively dispatch and support tow operators responding in the field. It is also important to note that a responding vehicle's total height may change based on whether the vehicle is loaded or not. Dispatchers and support staff should always think beyond the initial response and carefully consider the routes taken by units loaded with large equipment or vehicles post incident.

Similarly, a working knowledge of your area's emergency evacuation routes, and the main thoroughfares they connect to, is important during emergency and disaster response. These routes are designed to move people quickly and effectively from densely populated and/or potentially hazardous areas in the event of an emergency or disaster. During evacuation scenarios, traffic lights and roadway restrictions could be altered to assist in the flow of traffic in one direction. These roadways, and many of the lower volume streets feeding these systems, will most likely become highly congested and increase the risk of primary and secondary incidents. For obvious reasons, these factors can significantly change the landscape of a response initiative and should be carefully considered and anticipated.

The best way to learn your local geography is to get out on the road. Take some time to drive around, either on your own or with a fellow employee, and learn traffic patterns and road layout. Your fellow truck operators are an invaluable source of information. They are on the road at all times of day and experience firsthand how conditions change.

3.5.2 Weather

Weather can also play a significant role during an incident recovery. It can develop quickly and complicate even the simplest of recoveries. Heavy rainfall and snow can complicate recovery by reducing visibility and traction. Snow and rain can also increase regular traffic volume, making the field of operation more crowded and dangerous. A regular back up may double in size during inclement weather. Extreme heat can lead to dehydration and fatigue, while extreme cold can make safe operation more difficult.

Depending on the weather conditions, different resources may be required for a safe and efficient recovery. During warm weather, fluids and shade should be readily available. Because operators will fatigue faster, additional manpower may be needed. In reduced visibility scenarios like storms, additional reflective gear and lighting may be needed to ensure operators are safe on-scene.

3.5.3 Hazardous Materials

A hazardous material release also significantly changes an incident response. Any motor vehicle, regardless of size or classification, may be carrying hazardous materials. If a potential hazardous material release is identified, response actions should be halted, a trained HAZMAT response operator should be immediately notified, and corrective actions immediately taken. This may include, but not limited to, damming, diking, or diverting the hazardous material, deploying approved absorbent pads or spread, or activating an appropriate HAZMAT response unit for more serious incidents. Having situational awareness will allow you to identify potentially hazardous materials when arriving on-scene based on the vehicle and its markings. Being aware will allow faster and more effective response when a HAZMAT situation presents itself.

You can always work on your situational awareness. When you are out running errands or heading to or from the office, take a minute to notice any changes. Is there a new building going up? Did you see a recently opened construction zone? Perhaps you noticed a sign for an event that will shut down a main thoroughfare soon. If it is raining, take note of how traffic patterns change. You can save invaluable time and resources by recognizing these small variables and always remaining observant of your surroundings and local geography.

4 During the Incident

4.1 Stages of the Recovery Scene

Understanding the stages and activities of a recovery scene will help you support the operator and incident management (IM) partners on the scene. As you may recall from your National Traffic Incident Management (TIM) Responder Training (SHRP2)[3], the stages of a recovery scene are:

1. **Detection**- is the discovery of an incident and the first step in the TIM process. Incident detection can be a call from the parties involved in the incident, a call from a passing motorist, or by responders who happen upon them.

2. **Notification**- once detection and verification are complete, the communications center will dispatch the appropriate response.

3. **Arrival**- upon first arriving on-scene, an immediate arrival/windshield size-up report is conducted and relayed to later arriving units.

4. **Response Activities**- responders are working the scene according to TIM and quick clearance guidelines. For interdisciplinary incidents this will include establishing an Incident Command System (ICS). Medical care for injured motorists, HAZMAT containment, etc. also take place at this stage.

5. **Clearance & Termination**- Clearance is the removal of the obstruction from travel lanes. Termination is the final stage of incident response and includes demobilizing and removing all equipment, personnel and response vehicles, and restoring traffic flow to normal.

---

[3] (U.S. Department of Transportation Federal Highway Administration, 2017)

6. **Recovery**- the return of traffic flow to normal.

(U.S. Department of Transportation Federal Highway Administration, 2017)

4.2   Concurrent Tasks

Every responder has an important role to fill. As a support staff you may not be on-scene, but you still provide a valuable contribution to the recovery efforts. Understanding the basic functions of each on-scene IM partner during the stages of a recovery scene will help you in your role.

According to the U.S. Department of Transportation's Federal Highway Administration (FHWA)[4], the following are general actions taken by responders:

- **Emergency 911 Dispatchers**: Typically, the first to have knowledge of an incident, their goal is "to quickly, accurately, and completely convey the necessary information to the

---

[4] (U.S. Department of Transportation Federal Highway Administration, 2017)

proper agencies and field personnel to get the right personnel and equipment to the scene as quickly as possible".

- **Law Enforcement**: Often the first to arrive on the scene, "they assess the situation and call for additional resources (fire, EMS, and towing and recovery, among others) as needed. The officer secures the scene for responder and motorist safety, and conducts temporary traffic control as necessary. Law enforcement also conducts scene investigation and/or evidence collection as dictated by the incident scene and severity".

- **Fire and Rescue**: If arriving first on-scene, "they secure the scene to protect responders and motorists. Upon securing the scene, these personnel assess injured parties, and if warranted, request EMS support. Fire and rescue personnel provide first aid until EMS personnel arrive (if requested). Fire and rescue personnel address any fire or potential fire hazards and assist in scene recovery. In most locations, they also assess the scene for hazardous materials and notify remediation or clean-up contractors, as needed".

- **Emergency Medical Services (EMS)**: They "assess injuries, administer triage on-scene as needed, and remove injured parties quickly to medical facilities for additional care. In those areas of the country where EMS is a fire-based function, the fire and rescue personnel provide EMS functions".

- **Towing and Recovery**: "The towing and recovery personnel primarily remove disabled vehicles, clear incident debris, and clean up spilled cargo".

- **Transportation Agencies**: Traffic Management Centers (TMCs) "serve as the hub for the collection and dissemination of incident information and play a critical role with incident detection and verification. At the incident scene, transportation agency responders focus on temporary traffic control, expedite scene clearance, and restore traffic flow. Transportation agency responders include maintenance personnel and specialized traffic incident responders, such as maintenance and service patrol personnel".

4.3 Notification & Detection

As a towing and recovery support staff it is important to understand the notification and detection processes. You may be notified of an incident in one of several ways:

- **Customer Request**- vehicle owners/operators may contact you directly.

- **Police/Fire/Law Enforcement**- official notification and request for services from the municipal police department or other designated agency.

- **3rd Party Dispatch**- calls from motor clubs, dispatch companies, and emergency services (such as On-Star) may contact you directly.

With the improvement of technology, early detection of an incident is also getting easier. While it is important not to respond until notified by the appropriate channels, an advanced warning helps your tow operators prepare to respond.

- **Social Media**- depending on the severity of an incident, you may hear about an incident blocking the roadways on social media outlets for local news stations, etc.

- **City Cameras** or **Closed-Circuit Television Cameras (CCTV)**- if your community has cameras monitoring your roadways, these can be an early detection system.

4.4 Recovery Resources

4.4.1 Equipment

Equipment is one of the most obvious resources available to you during an incident recovery. A basic understanding of the function and capacity of towing and recovery equipment will help you coordinate tow operators with pending assignments and help incident scene management.

Sending the wrong equipment to a scene often results in lost time and frustration. Talk with your tow operator(s) about the equipment they use frequently.

- The term **tow truck** generally describes a vehicle engineered to hook up to the front or rear of another vehicle and move it. They come in various sizes and configurations depending on intended use. Some of the most common configurations include a wheel lift, which moves a vehicle by lifting its drive wheels off the ground allowing the vehicle to ride on its own suspension. Some tow trucks are manufactured with a recovery boom separate from the wheel lift. When the recovery boom and the wheel lift are built together it is called an integrated boom.

- **Flatbed trucks,** sometimes referred to as "rollbacks," feature a driver cab with a long flatbed behind it. A hydraulic system is used to raise and lower the bed for easy loading. The bed's ability to angle to the ground means that vehicles can be driven or pulled directly onto the bed and securely tied down. These trucks are some of the most common equipment used in the industry because of their ease of use, relative safety, and lack of moving parts.

- A **sliding axle trailer** is a trailer that connects to a road tractor for transport. It works in a similar way as a rollback. The axles slide forward, and the trailer can be raised with hydraulics, so it has the capability to be loaded from the ground. Most sliding axle trailers come with a winch to load equipment.

- A **lo-boy trailer** is a trailer that connects to a road tractor for transport. These trailers can haul taller equipment and detach towards the front of the trailer to load equipment from the ground.

- A **crane** is a type of machine, generally equipped with a hoist rope, wire, or chain that can be used both to lift and lower materials and to move them horizontally. A crane can be used to move heavy and/or oddly shaped equipment onto and into trucks, lift a vehicle that has rolled over, or move equipment around a facility. Note, a crane boom needs to be used at a higher boom angle for heavy lifting.

- A **rotator** is essentially a tow truck with crane capabilities. Rotators have the advantage of quick set-up and the boom can be used at a lower angle for recoveries.

- A **loader** is a machine used to move aside load materials such as asphalt, demolition debris, dirt, snow, gravel, rock, sand, woodchips, etc. These machines can also be equipped with various attachments used for moving vehicles, sweeping up materials, and storage devices like pallets. There are many types of loaders, which, depending on design and application, are called by various names, including bucket loader, front loader, front-end loader, payloader, scoop, shovel, skip loader, wheel loader, or skid-steer. Because of their many applications, they can play a pivotal role in incident response, cleanup, and lot management.

- **Bulldozers** are large tractors, most often fitted with tracks, which employ a large movable metal plate used to push and pull large quantities of material such as sand, snow, refuse, and rubble. Often, bulldozers are also equipped with a claw and/or bucket system for digging, scooping, and loosening material.

- **Dumpsters** are mobile garbage containers specially designed to store a high volume of waste material until their contents can be disposed of responsibly. Dumpsters come in a variety of sizes and styles. The size and style of the dumpster will determine the truck or equipment needed to move and empty it. In towing and recovery, dumpsters can be used in conjunction with other equipment for large incident clean-up.

- **Dump trucks** are used for transporting loose material (such as sand, gravel, or waste). A typical dump truck is equipped with an open-box bed, which is hinged at the rear and equipped with hydraulic rams to lift the front, allowing the material in the bed to be deposited or "dumped" behind the truck. They can be used in conjunction with other equipment to speed up incident clean up and transport equipment and materials.

- **Support unit** is a general term used to describe an additional unit carrying a variety of tools, equipment, and resources that may be required on-scene to facilitate the recovery effort.

4.4.2 Human Capital

Human capital is defined as the skills and experience within your colleagues. Human capital is just as important of a resource, if not more so, than equipment. Dispatching the correct person(s) to the recovery is critical to the success of the recovery. Some questions to ask yourself:

- Who is available right now to assist in this recovery?

- What is the skill level of my available operator(s)? Understanding the skill level of each tow operator will allow you to maximize the efficiency between dispatch, the towing operator, and IM partners.

- Do I need to call in a partner resource such as HAZMAT, Rapid Incident Scene Clearance (RISC) network partners, environmental clean-up companies, etc.?

Note, potential elements such as weather, local events, rush hour traffic, out-of-service equipment, etc. may impact the availability of resources (equipment and human).

4.5 Controlling the Communication

Support staff play a critical role in the communication surrounding an incident. Your ability to ask the right questions, get the required information, and relay that information impacts the abilities and performance of those on-scene who depend on that data.

One of the most important pieces of information to gather and relay is the incident's location. With each state and city having their own unique way of labeling streets and places, it is best to have a standard format for communicating the location. If possible, it's best practice to identify an incident's location by:

1. **Roadway**- What street the scene is on and a second street (or cross street) advising the vicinity. With some cities having street names that sound similar to one another, it might be best to have the street name spelled to you and a zip code. On interstates this will also include on or off-ramps, the lane, and the incident's location on either the shoulder or median (if applicable).

2. **Direction of travel**- When responding to a recovery scene on the interstate you'll need to communicate the direction of travel (Northbound, Southbound, Eastbound, Westbound). Sometimes responding to a scene will require an alternate or opposing direction lane response (i.e. driving the wrong way on a roadway). Given the significant safety concerns implied, it is important that you have all the pertinent information and know the agency protocols in these situations.

3. **Any landmarks or mile markers**- landmarks and/or mile markers fine tune the location for the responder. Landmarks can be naturally occurring such as hills, fields, and ditches or manmade such as bridges, shopping centers, intersections, and unique buildings.

4.6   NIMS and ICS

Developed by the Department of Homeland Security, the **National Incident Management System (NIMS)** is a set of best practices for responders at all jurisdictional levels and across all disciplines to allow for more efficient and effective cooperation. One of the most valuable

organizational processes set in NIMS is the **Incident Command System (ICS)** [5]. The ICS is the

standardized organizational structure for the management of incidents. The concepts covered by

ICS include common terminology, integrated communication, management by objectives, Unified

Command, the Chain of Command, the establishment/transfer of command, and more.

The Incident Commander (IC) is the person responsible for all aspects of an IM response

including "establishing objectives, planning strategies, and implementing tactics"[6]. Typically, the IC

will be a law enforcement or fire responder depending on the incident type. However, on a small

incident, one person, such as the tow operator, may serve as the IC and only responder. On

intermediate or major incidents, the IC is responsible for delegating to Command Staff who support

the duties of the Command such as the Public Information Officer, Safety Officer, and Liaison

Officer.

Once established by the first responder, the IC may change under several circumstances[7]:

- If a more qualified person arrives from the same agency as the acting IC

- The priority changes requiring control by a different agency with functional or
  jurisdictional responsibility

- If the IC position is specified by law or agreement

- The incident decreases in complexity to a level where a less qualified on-scene
  responder from the same agency can now control the situation

- When the acting IC needs to be relieved by a comparable on-scene responder after
  an extended incident duration

---

[5] (Federal Emergency Management Agency, 2004)
[6] (FEMA Emergency Management Institute, 2008)
[7] (Federal Highway Administration, 2006)

NIMS and ICS are complex and cannot be covered thoroughly here. For this reason, we recommend all support staff complete courses on these important subjects. FEMA's Emergency Management Institute offers a variety of courses, visit their website for more information: https://training.fema.gov/nims/.

4.7   Safety

Safety is a primary concern for on and off-scene responders across all IM disciplines. Several factors can impact the safety of responders on-scene and those in the vicinity.

Weather can pose a significant safety concern especially extreme cold or heat. These conditions carry additional protection needs for the responders. Hydration and awareness of heat are key safety factors during extreme heat conditions. During extreme cold conditions adequate clothing for warmth is critical. Extra caution needs to be taken to prevent slip and fall injuries on slippery surfaces.

Traffic control conditions at the scene can also pose a safety hazard. These conditions could be improper early incident scene warning devices, excessive apparatus lighting, gaps in staged traffic control units, improper positioning of responder vehicles, and extended scene clearance.

Another safety factor to consider is the overall **congestion at the scene** of various responders. To minimize congestion unnecessary equipment, resources, and personnel should be released from the scene when their work is completed. Every effort should be made to produce a safe, expedited clearing of the incident scene as this is the best way to protect all responders.

When working in off-road or light obscured **terrains**, close proximity power lines can become an issue, especially when it is necessary to cut down trees to complete a recovery. It is critical a scene is walked, checked, and declared all-clear before the recovery begins. Rough terrain also requires special care to avoid responders tripping and falling on rocks, into holes, or down slopes. Heavy foliage can conceal these safety hazards.

The presenting, possibly unstable, **position of a causality** can affect safety. Special care needs to be taken to properly assess the stability and condition of vehicles impacted in the incident. Vehicles that are rolled-over or overturned are of special concern and can collapse on responders if not properly secured. In incidents involving cargo, shifting during handling can become a crush injury to a responder. Batteries should be disconnected upon arrival to protect against potential fire hazards.

Hazardous materials may also be present at an incident scene. Every effort should be made to properly identify cargo through the bill of lading, fleet contact or visual inspection, unless placards are visible. If placards are visible, proper Emergency Response Guidebook (ERG) protocol should be followed. Responders and support staff should familiarize themselves with the visual recognition of tankers and trailers that are prevalent in HAZMAT transport in case placards are missing or obscured post incident.

According to the Federal Motor Carrier Safety Administration (FMCSA), there are nine (9) categories of hazardous materials: 1) Explosives, 2) Gases, 3) Flammable Liquid and Combustible Liquid, 4) Flammable Solid, Spontaneously Combustible and Dangerous When Wet 5) Oxidizer and Organic Peroxide, 6) Poison (Toxic) and Poison Inhalation Hazard, 7) Radioactive, 8) Corrosive, and 9) Miscellaneous[8]. One of the easiest ways to identify if a hazardous material is present is to look for a placard. If a hazardous material is identified on-scene, you can quickly identify the material and emergency procedures using the Pipeline and Hazardous Materials Safety Administration's (PHMSA) Emergency Response Guidebook (ERG). Physical guides are available, and we

---

[8] (Federal Motor Carrier Safety Administration, 2013)

recommend downloading the free ERG 2016 Mobile App available for Android and Apple phones[9].

Visit the ERG website for more information: https://www.phmsa.dot.gov/hazmat/erg/emergency-response-guidebook-erg.

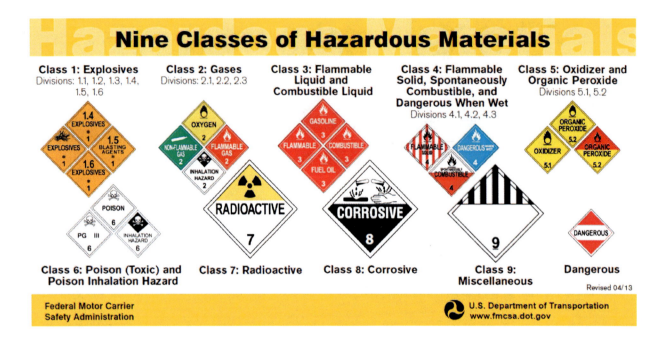

Hazardous materials can pose a threat not only on-scene, but wherever the vehicle goes next such as a storage lot. For this reason, employees who may be exposed to a vehicle post incident should also be aware of hazardous materials and safety protocols. If vehicles containing hazardous materials are stored at a company lot, the advice of a HAZMAT specialist is recommended to determine the best process for storage.

A vehicle may be carrying **freight** when it is involved in an incident. Freight or cargo is generally classified as perishable (food grade), hard line goods (steel, machinery), virgin goods (plastic beads, base products for product), controlled commodities (mail, fire arms, FDA loads), bulk loads (petroleum, grain), or HAZMAT (fuels, chemicals). Handling of these goods on-scene can determine their condition post incident. If the cargo cannot be utilized for its original purpose it will

[9] (ERG2016 MobileApp, 2017)

not be redeemable. The FDA Food Safety Modernization Act (FSMA) provides guidelines for a myriad of cargo.

At an incident, the **Safety Officer** is responsible for monitoring on-scene operations and advising the IC on matters related to the safety and health of responders. The ICS Safety Officer even has the authority to put an emergency stop on the recovery activities in the event of unsafe actions[10]. The Safety Officer is responsible for ensuring that all responders are wearing appropriate **personal protective equipment (PPE)** such as ANSI compliant high visibility garments, hard hats, safety glasses, gloves, proper footwear, and supplied air respirators (SCBA) as required by conditions. Additional duties include documentation of the recovery, time records, breakdown and clearing of equipment and personnel, and the wrap-up of scene clearing with the IC.

4.8   Communication: Who, What, When, & How

Clear and concise communication is required during an active incident recovery. In order to communicate effectively you will need to understand the who, what, when, and how of communication during this period.

During an active recovery you can expect to receive a number of **external calls** ranging from private customers, insurance companies, brokerage companies, etc. When dealing with these external callers, your first priority is to reassure and inform them as appropriate. Take a message from the caller including his or her contact information, insurance information, and any photographs that may have been taken of the vehicle or incident. This information will be vital when you are communicating with them post incident.

---

[10] (Federal Emergency Management Agency, 2012)

If the caller is notifying you of an incident, you will need to get additional information from them such as a description of the vehicle, call back number, and the number of passengers currently in the vehicle. The Wisconsin Statewide Traffic Incident Management Enhancement (TIME) Program has created a **Towing and Recovery Call-Out Checklist**[11] that is particularly useful for these types of calls.

During an incident recovery, off-scene support staff should have periodic and planned communication with the on-scene responders or designated company point person (if available). In order to protect the safety of the on-scene responder it is important to only contact them for an external customer service inquiry when it is absolutely essential. Otherwise, wait until the scheduled update interval.

To understand the situation on-scene, and support the on-scene responders, you should ask the following questions during your periodic check-in:

- ☐ Has the scene changed?

- ☐ What are the current scene conditions?

- ☐ Are additional resources needed?

- ☐ What is the current state of command?

- ☐ Is cargo present?

- ☐ Are there any hazardous materials present?

- ☐ Estimated time to completion based on the recovery plan?

---

[11] (Wisconsin Department of Transportation, 2014)

For intermediate or major incidents with multiple Command Staff present, it is important to communicate with the IC and your company's designated responder or company scene manager (if applicable).

4.9   Physiological Considerations

On-scene responders can work in physically demanding conditions for hours on end. In order to support them in their recovery efforts, it is important to understand some of the physiological considerations at play.

While responders often like to push themselves, they are only human. Access to basic needs such as food, water, and bathroom facilities can be limited during a recovery scene. Fatigue, exhaustion, and other conditions can also play a role depending on the circumstances.

- **Fatigue**- According to the Occupational Safety & Health Administration (OSHA), the "symptoms of fatigue, both mental and physical, vary and depend on the person and his or her degree of overexertion" and include: weariness, sleepiness, irritability, reduced alertness, lack of concentration and memory, and headache[12].

- **Heat Exhaustion**- "Heat exhaustion is the body's response to loss of water and salt from heavy sweating. Signs include headache, nausea, dizziness, weakness, irritability, and thirst". Symptoms also include vomiting, lightheadedness, and a fast heartbeat[13].

- **Heat Stroke**- Heat stroke is the most serious form of heat-related illness. This happens "when the body becomes unable to regulate its core temperature. Sweating stops and the body can no longer rid itself of excess heat. Heat stroke is a medical

---

[12] (Occupational Safety & Health Administration, n.d.)
[13] (Occupational Safety & Health Administration, n.d.)

emergency that may result in death! Call 911 immediately". Symptoms include

confusion, fainting, seizures, loss of consciousness, and red, hot, dry skin[14].

- **Hypothermia**- Hypothermia "occurs when body heat is lost faster than it can be

  replaced and the normal body temperature (98.6°F) drops to less than 95°F.

  Hypothermia is most likely at very cold temperatures, but it can occur even at cool

  temperatures (above 40°F), if a person becomes chilled from rain, sweat, or

  submersion in cold water". Symptoms include shivering, stomping their feet to

  generate heat, confusion, lack of hand eye coordination, disorientation, dilated

  pupils, and slowed breathing. If you suspect a responder may be suffering from

  hypothermia instruct them to move to a warm/dry place, remove/replace any wet

  clothes, and call 911 immediately[15].

- **Frostbite**- "Frostbite is an injury to the body that is caused by freezing of the skin

  and underlying tissues. The lower the temperature, the more quickly frostbite will

  occur. Frostbite typically affects the extremities, particularly the feet and hands.

  Amputation may be required in severe cases". Symptoms include reddened skin

  developing gray and white patches, numbness in the affected part, skin feels firm or

  hard, and blisters may occur in severe cases[16]. If you suspect a responder may be

  suffering from hypothermia instruct them to move to a warm/dry place,

  remove/replace any wet clothes, and call 911 immediately[17].

All these conditions are serious. As a support staff it is important to be aware of the warning

signs and understand the appropriate action to be taken if any of the on-scene responders start

---

[14] (Occupational Safety & Health Administration, n.d.)
[15] (Occupational & Safety Health Administration, n.d.)
[16] (Occupational & Safety Health Administration, n.d.)
[17] (Occupational & Safety Health Administration, n.d.)

exhibiting symptoms. To minimize the risk, on-scene responders should be monitored and rotated during extended recoveries.

4.10 Multiple Calls

Given the nature of the towing industry, multiple incidents can occur simultaneously or in rapid succession. It is also not uncommon for a major incident to cause secondary crashes on the roadway. During this influx of service demands, support staff play a significant role. You must remain calm and focused.

Support staff will need to clearly record the vital information for each call, so they can accurately evaluate the severity of the call, equipment needed, staff resources and in what order to dispatch the calls if resources are limited. Support staff should utilize a Towing & Recovery Call Checklist, such as the Wisconsin DOT's[18], to minimize missing or misrepresented information. Additionally, support staff should be familiar with the company's equipment, the equipment's capabilities, staff and their specialized skills.

Priority calls would include those that block traffic, compromise the safety of the victims and other first responders on-scene, HAZMAT scenes, a declared state of emergency, entrapment or fatality. **Secondary calls** would include service calls, minor incidents, or a breakdown without injury.

The company's scene supervisor should be made aware of the calls in progress or in need of dispatch. As resources are no longer needed at a priority scene, they can be redirected to expedite service elsewhere.

---

[18] (Wisconsin Department of Transportation, 2014)

4.11 Dismissing Equipment

The goal of the recovery team is to utilize their collective knowledge and actions to produce a safe, expedited recovery and restoration of the incident scene. The towing operator is particularly focused on the safe, effective, and expedient removal of the vehicle(s). Removing the vehicle obstructing the roadway re-establishes traffic flow and minimizes the exposure of the responders to roadway hazards.

According to NIMS, only equipment and personnel necessary to the productive mitigation of the incident should be at the scene. When equipment and personnel have completed their service needs, they should be dismissed. Every effort should be made to avoid an over congested scene since congestion and overcrowding pose safety hazards.

On-scene responders should maintain time logs for each piece of equipment and operator. Photos of the incident and recovery should also be taken. This documentation is key for the protection of the company and billing preparation.

5   Post Incident

5.1   Post Incident Assessment

The goal of a post incident assessment after an intermediate or major incident is to improve on-scene performance for next time. This is an opportunity to review the successes and failures of that particular incident and make any appropriate adjustments. If possible, a post incident review with multiple incident management (IM) disciplines is best. All aspects of the incident are to be discussed including the overall process, time frame, potential alternative approaches, any inherent dangers given the incident, the performance of each task, and objective metrics. Metrics to review include:

- Was the correct information gathered during notification?

- Was the information effectively relayed to the team?

- Efficiency of time response to the scene against established goals.

- Quality of communication between team members.

- Overall clearance times.

- Were the correct decisions made and directives given?

- Post incident dissemination of documentation to proper parties i.e. customer, agency, company administrators, etc.

The benefits of post incident assessments, sometimes known as critical incident reviews (CIRs), are[19]:

- The opportunity for responders to discuss an incident together in a no-fault atmosphere.

- Improving safety and clearance times at incident scenes.

---

[19] (PB Farradyne, 2005)

- An effective tool to identify areas of improvement and confirm the value of good practices through a meeting of responders shortly after a major incident occurs.

- A means to help in developing and maintaining lines of communication and relationships among agencies.

- Coordinated enhancements to the activities of the TIM teams through use of the lessons learned and articulated in the course of CIRs.

5.2   Customer Service: Post Incident

While the incident may be over, and the roadway cleared, your interaction with the customer continues. As a towing and recovery support staff you need to be able to communicate post incident procedures with external customers such as insurance companies, independent auto damage appraisers, leasing companies, car rental companies, lien holders, vehicle owners and their families. They will want to know what the next steps for the vehicle will be and what options are available to them (if any).

Please refer to your city, state, or municipality requirements and/or limitations of notification. It is important that the company, and you as the support staff, do not divulge information to the wrong individual or entity. You must follow the regulations in your area and respect the privacy of the vehicle owner. The vehicle owner is your customer.

When interacting with insurance companies and auto damage appraisers, it is important to maintain the owner's rights and those of the towing company. It is vital that you understand and abide by your company's policies and legal requirements when interacting with external customers. In many instances, companies require completed direction-to-pay and hold-harmless forms on file. You may only have one opportunity to secure these documents.

The vehicle owner, or the delegated financial party, should receive a well formatted billing presentation with an overview of the incident including photos. If a directive is given to deliver or move a vehicle to a repair facility or some other location, support staff should confirm the directive with the vehicle owner or the delegated party of representation. It is best practice to get the receiving party's information and documentation of receipt of the vehicle. Potential next steps for a recovered vehicle include:

- **Repair**- The vehicle may be repairable. Outline the options to the customer. A good practice is to educate the customer of his/her rights for repair as outlined by your state consumer affairs. If your company is a mechanical or auto body repair facility, this is a good opportunity to promote your business.

- **Total Loss**- The vehicle may be determined a total loss either by the insurance company or in the case of an uninsured vehicle, based on the damage resulting from the incident. In this case, you will need to outline the options to the customer.

  o **Fully Insured Vehicle** - If the vehicle is fully insured and deemed a total loss, the insurance company should be responsible for payment of the towing and storage fees. This is where the life cycle of the vehicle may vary. Based on the value of the vehicle, it may be transferred to an insurance salvage lot for auction. It is important that the towing company obtain a release from the vehicle owner and that the owner has removed all personal property.

  o **Uninsured/Underinsured Vehicle** - If the vehicle has no salvage value, the insurance company may opt out of responsibility for the scrap vehicle. In this case, the owner may have the option of retaining possession of the vehicle or selling it outright. Please refer to your company policy regarding underinsured or uninsured vehicles. In many cases the vehicle owner may be responsible for the towing and storage charges owed to the towing company.

- **Drivable**- The vehicle may have sustained minimal damage as a result of the incident. If the vehicle appears drivable, you should advise the vehicle owner to have the vehicle checked for any hidden damage.

5.3   Shadowing & Interdisciplinary Learning

It is important to familiarize yourself with incident recovery from the prospective of the towing operator and our IM partners. Support staff should periodically perform a "ride along", or shadow, to attain a full understanding of the methodology and responsibilities of the different disciplines on-scene and their specific rolls. It is important to do this regularly, even if you've done one in the past, as best practices, technology, and techniques change. You must stay up-to-date for the purposes of safety, more efficient methods and equipment. The better you can understand the activities of a towing operator or IM partner on-scene the better you'll be able to anticipate their needs, interpret their environment remotely, and support them in the recovery effort.

Hands-on trainings and mock incidents with several different disciplines will continue to improve the team effort. Some support staff, such as dispatchers, rarely have the opportunity to be on-scene and attain a firsthand understanding of an incident. This off-scene staff needs to have the ability to "paint the picture" of the incident they are working using the information relayed in the size-up from on-scene responders. Communications should be clear and concise with the necessary information available, so the dispatcher can be prepared for upcoming needs before the incident completion. Having all participants sharing the same available information only improves team performance.

The benefits of shadowing do not end with the tow operator. Our partners in fire, police, EMS, 911 dispatch, DOT, public works, etc. all have a critical role to play in clearing the roadways. Understanding the resources and procedures of our incident management partners can prove invaluable in performing your own duties. Get involved in your local IM community. If a partner is hosting a training event, see if you can participate. At the least, periodically spend time shadowing other disciplines. Invite IM partners to shadow you for a day. Strengthening the lines of communication and understanding each other's prospective makes everyone better.

6 Glossary of Terms

Term	Description
ANSI	American National Standards Institute (ANSI) is a premier source for timely, relevant, actionable information on national, regional, international standards and conformity assessment issues (American National Standards Institute, 2018).
Department of Homeland Security (DHS)	The Department of Homeland Security works to improve the security of the United States. The Department's work includes customs, border, and immigration enforcement, emergency response to natural and manmade disasters, antiterrorism work, and cybersecurity (U.S. Department of Homeland Security, 2018).
Department of Transportation (DOT)	The Department of Transportation is responsible for planning and coordinating federal transportation projects. It also sets safety regulations for all major modes of transportation (U.S. Department of Transportation, 2018).
Emergency 911 Dispatchers	A 911 dispatcher coordinates emergency responder, including police, fire, EMS, and towing, to provide quick responses to emergencies.
Emergency Response Guidebook (ERG)	A guidebook written by the U.S. Department of Transportation's Pipeline and Hazardous Materials Safety Administration (PHMSA) and intended for use by first responders during the initial phase of a transportation incident involving dangerous goods/hazardous materials (Pipeline and Hazardous Materials Safety Administration, 2018).
FDA Food Safety Modernization Act (FSMA)	The U.S. Food & Drug Administration's Food Safety Modernization Act (a) enables the FDA to better protect public health by strengthening the food safety and (b) enables FDA to focus more on preventing food safety problems rather than relying primarily on reacting to problems after they occur. The provides FDA with new enforcement authorities and new tools to hold imported foods to the same standards as domestic foods and directs FDA to build an integrated national food safety system in partnership with state and local authorities (Background on the FDA Food Safety Modernization Act, 2018).
Federal Highway Administration (FHWA)	FHWA is an agency within the U.S. Department of Transportation that supports state and local governments in the design, construction, and maintenance of the Nation's highway system and various federally and tribal owned lands (Understanding Federal Highway Administration (FHWA), 2018).
Federal Motor Carrier Safety Administration (FMCSA)	Federal Motor Carrier Safety Administration the lead federal government agency responsible for regulating and providing safety oversight of commercial motor vehicles (CMVs). FMCSA's mission is to reduce crashes, injuries, and fatalities involving large trucks and buses. FMCSA partners with industry, safety advocates, and state and local governments to roadways safe and improve CMV safety through regulation, education, enforcement, research, and technology (Who We Are, 2018).
FEMA's Emergency Management Institute (EMI)	EMI's purpose is to support the Department of Homeland Security and FEMA's goals by improving the competencies of the U.S. officials in Emergency Management at all levels of government to prepare for, protect against, respond to, recover from, and mitigate the potential effects of all types of disasters and emergencies on the American people (Emergency Management Institute, 2018).

Hazardous Materials (HAZMAT)	DOT defines a hazardous material as any item or chemical which, when being transported or moved in commerce, is a risk to public safety or the environment, and is regulated as such under its Pipeline and Hazardous Materials Safety Administration regulations (49 CFR 100-199), which includes the Hazardous Materials Regulations (49 CFR 171-180). In addition, hazardous materials in transport are regulated by the International Maritime Dangerous Goods Code; Dangerous Goods Regulations of the International Air Transport Association; Technical Instructions of the International Civil Aviation Organization; and U.S. Air Force Joint Manual, Preparing Hazardous Materials for Military Air Shipments (What are Hazardous Materials?, 2018).
Liaison Officer	The LNO is the point of contact for representatives of other governmental agencies, nongovernmental organizations, and/or private entities. In either a single or Unified Command structure, representatives from assisting or cooperating agencies and organizations coordinate through the LNO (Lesson 4: Functional Areas & Positions, 2018).
Insurance Adjusters	Insurance adjusters investigate, analyze, and determine the extent of insurance company's liability concerning personal, casualty, or property loss or damages, and attempt to effect settlement with claimants. Correspond with or interview medical specialists, agents, witnesses, or claimants to compile information. Calculate benefit payments and approve payment of claims within a certain monetary limit (Insurance Adjusters, Examiners, and Investigators Job Description, 2018).
National Highway Traffic Safety Administration (NHTSA)	The National Highway Traffic Safety Administration is responsible for keeping people safe on America's roadways. NHTSA reduces deaths, injuries and economic losses from motor vehicle crashes through enforcing vehicle performance standards and partnerships with state and local governments (About NHTSA, 2018).
National Incident Management System (NIMS)	NIMS is a comprehensive, national approach to incident management that is applicable at all jurisdictional levels and across functional disciplines. It is intended to: • Be applicable across a full spectrum of potential incidents, hazards, and impacts, regardless of size, location or complexity. • Improve coordination and cooperation between public and private entities in a variety of incident management activities. • Provide a common standard for overall incident management. (U.S. Department of Homeland Security, 2018)
Public Information Officer (PIO)	The PIO is responsible for interfacing with the public and media and/or with other agencies with incident-related information requirements. The PIO develops accurate and complete information on the incident's cause, size, and current situation; resources committed; and other matters of general interest for both internal and external consumption. The PIO may also perform a key public information-monitoring role (Lesson 4: Functional Areas & Positions, 2018).
Rapid Incident Scene Clearance (RISC)	The Rapid Incident Scene Clearance (RISC) Program is an initiative that contracts towing companies to provide quick, safe clearance of large vehicle crashes, such as tractor trailers, box trucks, and boats that are overturned or damaged to the point where the vehicle cannot be towed by a smaller tow truck on the interstate (FDOT District 2 , 2018).

Safety Officer	The SO monitors incident operations and advises the Incident Commander on all matters relating to operational safety, including the health and safety of emergency responder personnel. The SO is responsible to the Incident Commander for the set of systems and procedures necessary to ensure ongoing assessment of hazardous environments, coordination of multiagency safety efforts, and implementation of measures to promote emergency responder safety, as well as the general safety of incident operations (Lesson 4: Functional Areas & Positions, 2018).
Situational Awareness	Situational awareness is being aware of what is happening around you in terms of where you are, where you are supposed to be, and whether anyone or anything around you is a threat to your health and safety (Health and Safety in the Construction Industry, 2018).
Supplied Air Respirators (SCBA)	SCBA are an atmosphere-supplying respirator for which the breathing air source is designed to be carried by the user (Occupational Safety and Health Administration, 2018).
Traffic Management Centers (TMCs)	TMCs are the hub of a traffic control system. The TMC brings together human and technological components from various agencies to perform a variety of functions. TMCs may deal with freeway traffic management, surface street traffic management, transit management or some combination of these functions (Federal Highway Administration, 2018).
Winching	A device for hauling or lifting; made up of a rope, cable or chain wound around a horizontal rotating drum and turned by a crank or motor and typically mounted at the rear of a towing vehicle (McBratney, 2015).

7 References

About NHTSA. (2018, May). Retrieved from National Highway Traffic Safety Administration: https://www.nhtsa.gov/about-nhtsa

American National Standards Institute. (2018, March). *ANSI Standards Subscription.* Retrieved from https://webstore.ansi.org/sdo_sitelicense/ansi.aspx

Background on the FDA Food Safety Modernization Act. (2018, March). Retrieved from U.S. Food & Drug Administration: https://www.fda.gov/NewsEvents/PublicHealthFocus/ucm239907.htm

Emergency Management Institute. (2018, March). Retrieved from Federal Emergency Management Agency: https://training.fema.gov/emi.aspx

ERG2016 MobileApp. (2017, December 8). Retrieved February 12, 2018, from https://www.phmsa.dot.gov/hazmat/erg/erg2016-mobileapp

FDOT District 2 . (2018, March). *Rapid Incident Scent Clearance (RISC)* . Retrieved from Traffic Incident Management: http://www.jax511.com/D2TIMwp/risc/

Federal Emergency Management Agency. (2004, November 23). *NIMS and the Incident Command System.* Retrieved February 7, 2018, from FEMA.gov: https://www.fema.gov/txt/nims/nims_ics_position_paper.txt

Federal Emergency Management Agency. (2012). *Position Qualifications for Operational Coordination: Incident Management.*

Federal Highway Administration. (2006). *Simplified Guide to the Incident Command System for Transportation Professionals.* Washington DC.

Federal Highway Administration. (2018, March). *Traffic Control Systems Handbook: Chapter 8. System Control* . Retrieved from https://ops.fhwa.dot.gov/publications/fhwahop06006/chapter_8.htm

Federal Motor Carrier Safety Administration. (2013, April). Retrieved 2 2018, from FMCSA: https://www.fmcsa.dot.gov/regulations/enforcement/nine-classes-hazardous-materials-yellow-visor-card

FEMA Emergency Management Institute. (2008, November). ICS-100: ICS for Higher Education—Student Manual. Retrieved from Emergency Management Institute.

Health and Safety in the Construction Industry. (2018, March). Retrieved from Health and Safety Executive: http://www.hse.gov.uk/construction/lwit/assets/downloads/situational-awareness.pdf

Insurance Adjusters, Examiners, and Investigators Job Description. (2018, March). Retrieved from InsuranceJobs.com: http://www.insurancejobs.com/insurance-adjusters-examiners-investigators-job-description.htm

Lesson 4: Functional Areas & Positions. (2018, March). Retrieved from FEMA.gov: https://emilms.fema.gov/IS200b/ICS0104summary.htm

McBratney, K. (2015, November 20). *What's a winch (and how it works).* Retrieved from Honk For Help: https://www.honkforhelp.com/explore/2015/whats-a-winch-and-how-it-works/

National Highway Traffic Safety Administration. (2015). *Traffic Safety Facts 2015.* Washington, DC.

Occupational & Safety Health Administration. (n.d.). *Cold Stress Guide.* Retrieved February 2018, from https://www.osha.gov/SLTC/emergencypreparedness/guides/cold.html

Occupational Safety & Health Administration. (n.d.). *Extended Unusual Work Shifts.* Retrieved February 2018, from https://www.osha.gov/OshDoc/data_Hurricane_Facts/faq_longhours.html

Occupational Safety & Health Administration. (n.d.). *Heat-related Illnesses and First Aid.* Retrieved February 2018, from https://www.osha.gov/SLTC/heatstress/heat_illnesses.html

Occupational Safety and Health Administration. (2018, March). *Section VIII: Chapter 2.* Retrieved from U.S. Department of Labor: https://www.osha.gov/dts/osta/otm/otm_viii/otm_viii_2.html

PB Farradyne. (2005, June). *Critical Incident Reviews: Technical Memorandum.* Retrieved February 7, 2018, from I-95 Corridor Coalition: http://i95coalition.org/projects/incident-management-library/

Pipeline and Hazardous Materials Safety Administration. (2018, March). *Emergency Response Guidebook (ERG) 2016.* Retrieved from https://www.phmsa.dot.gov/sites/phmsa.dot.gov/files/docs/ERG2016.pdf

Towing and Recovery Association of America, Inc. (2014). Law Enforcement Vehicle Identification Guide. Washington, DC.

U.S. Department of Homeland Security. (2018, March). Retrieved from USA.gov: https://www.usa.gov/federal-agencies/u-s-department-of-homeland-security

U.S. Department of Homeland Security. (2018, March). *NIMS: FREQUENTLY ASKED QUESTIONS.* Retrieved from FEMA.gov: https://www.fema.gov/pdf/emergency/nims/nimsfaqs.pdf

U.S. Department of Transportation. (2018, March). Retrieved from USA.gov: https://www.usa.gov/federal-agencies/u-s-department-of-transportation

U.S. Department of Transportation Federal Highway Administration. (2017, March). National Traffic Incident Management (TIM) Responder Training Program. *4-Hour Course Handbook.* Washington, DC.

U.S. Department of Transportation Federal Highway Administration. (2017, February 1). *TIM Tactical Program Elements.* Retrieved February 6, 2018, from https://ops.fhwa.dot.gov/eto_tim_pse/publications/timhandbook/chap3.htm

Understanding Federal Highway Administration (FHWA). (2018, March). Retrieved from Transportation.gov: https://www.transportation.gov/transition/FHWA/Understanding-FHWA

United States Department of Homeland Security. (2018, March). Retrieved from Wikipedia: https://en.wikipedia.org/wiki/United_States_Department_of_Homeland_Security

What are Hazardous Materials? (2018, March). Retrieved from Institute of Hazardous Materials Management: https://www.ihmm.org/about-ihmm/what-are-hazardous-materials

What Does a 911 Dispatcher Do? (2018, March). Retrieved from Learning.org: https://learn.org/articles/What_Does_a_911_Dispatcher_Do.html

Who We Are. (2018, March). Retrieved from Federal Motor Carrier Safety Administration: https://www.fmcsa.dot.gov/mission/who

Wisconsin Department of Transportation. (2014, November). *Emergency Traffic Control and Scene Management Guidelines.* Retrieved February 2018, from http://wisconsindot.gov/Pages/about-wisdot/who-we-are/dtsd/bto/stoc/time-guidelines.aspx

8   About the Author

The Towing and Recovery Association of America, Inc.® (TRAA) is the "The Voice of America's Towing Industry"! Founded in 1979 in Kansas City, Missouri TRAA is the umbrella trade group and national voice of the towing and recovery industry, which is estimated to include more than 35,000 towing businesses in the United States. TRAA's membership includes professionals from the United States, Canada, and abroad.

TRAA is a 501 (c)(6) nonprofit membership national towing association, governed by a representative board of directors whose officers are elected from the membership.

TRAA represents the interests of the towing and recovery industry on Capitol Hill, sponsoring annual events and meetings that are attended by members as well as state association officers and leaders. TRAA also produces an array of educational products supporting professionalism in towing and recovery and in business management.

Made in United States
North Haven, CT
28 April 2024

51858049R10031